Leading

SpiritBuilt Leadership 3

Malcolm Webber

Published by:

Strategic Press
www.StrategicPress.org

Strategic Press is a division of Strategic Global Assistance, Inc.
www.sgai.org

513 S. Main St. Suite 2
Elkhart, IN 46516
U.S.A.

+1-844-532-3371 (LEADER-1)

Copyright © 2003 Malcolm Webber

ISBN 978-1-888810-41-7

All Scripture references are from the New International Version of the Bible, unless otherwise noted.

Printed in the United States of America

Table of Contents

Introduction 7

1. What Leaders Do 9
2. Leaders See the Vision 13
3. Leaders Share the Vision 31
4. Leaders Shift the Vision 45
5. Leaders Show the Vision 61
6. Leaders Sustain the Vision 71

Introduction

In a previous book[1] we defined "leadership" in the following way: A leader helps someone move from where he is now to somewhere else.

But what do leaders actually do to cause this to happen?

In this book we will examine the practices of effective leaders.

In preparation please complete the following exercise.

---

[1] Please see *Leadership: SpiritBuilt Leadership #1* by Malcolm Webber.

EXERCISE

Think of a time when you watched a successful leader in action over a period of time.

What exactly did he or she do to cause the people to follow?

Please identify the practices of good leadership. What exactly do good leaders do? List their actions below:

_____

_____

_____

_____

_____

_____

_____

_____

_____

_____

chapter 1

What Leaders Do

According to our definition of leadership, a leader helps someone move from where he is now to somewhere else – preferably to somewhere better.

As we have previously seen,[2] there are three parts to this:

1. The leader establishes the direction.
2. He aligns the people in that direction.
3. He motivates and inspires them to move and keep moving in that direction until they fulfill the vision.

In achieving this, there are five fundamental practices of exemplary transformational leaders.[3] This is what leaders actually do in accomplishing the "helping someone move." When they are at their best, effective leaders:

1. See the vision. Leaders challenge the status quo, taking risks to fulfill the high calling of God.
2. Share the vision. Leaders capture the hearts of their followers with a passionate vision for the glory of God.
3. Shift the vision. Leaders build teams that will act on the vision.
4. Show the vision. Leaders validate the integrity of the vision to their constituents by personally setting the example and by planning small wins to demonstrate that the vision will work.

---

[2] Please see *Leadership: SpiritBuilt Leadership #1* by Malcolm Webber.
[3] These five practices of exemplary leaders follow, albeit somewhat loosely, the five leadership practices of Kouzes and Posner's *The Leadership Challenge (1995)*. In addition, some of our suggestions for improvement are adapted from their book, *Leadership Practices Inventory: Participants Workbook*.

5. Sustain the vision. Leaders strengthen the hearts of their people by keeping the people focused on the ultimate goal, by affirming them and their contributions and by celebrating their accomplishments.

This fits our three-part definition of leadership:

The leader starts where the people are now and he challenges the status quo with a new vision of possibility (practice 1). Next he shows the people where they could go (practice 2). He establishes the new direction and aligns the people with it (practice 2). Then he empowers, motivates and inspires them to move and to keep on moving in that direction to fulfill the vision (practices 3-5).

These five practices of exemplary leaders are summarized in the following table:

Summary of the Five Practices of Exemplary Leaders

Practice	What the leader does	The leader's actions related to the vision	The leader's actions related to the people	The leader's actions related to the three parts of leadership
1 Fire-starters	The leader goes to the mountain with God, dreams dreams and sees visions of the future.	Sees the vision	Clearly sees their future potential and purpose.	1
2 Fire-throwers	The leader comes down from the mountain and shares the vision he's seen with his people in such a way that they clearly see it and passionately own it.	Shares the vision	Engages their hearts with the vision of their own futures.	2
3 Fire-builders	The leader builds a team that will take responsibility for practically acting on the vision and bringing it to pass.	Shifts the vision	Builds them into a team and enables them to act on the vision and make it happen.	3
4 Fire-eaters	The leader demonstrates that the vision will work by personally modeling it and by starting with small wins.	Shows the vision	Sets them the example of his own model and builds credibility that the vision will work.	3

		Summary of the Five Practices of Exemplary Leaders		
Practice	What the leader does	The leader's actions related to the vision	The leader's actions related to the people	The leader's actions related to the three parts of leadership
5 Fire-stokers	The leader encourages the people to pursue the vision by focusing on the ultimate goal, by recognizing contributions and by celebrating accomplishments.	Sustains the vision	Strengthens and encourages them to continue to act and ultimately bring the vision for their futures to pass.	3

chapter 2

Leaders See the Vision

Good Christian leaders go for God's highest! They challenge the status quo. They pray and search for new opportunities.

God created the universe – there is nothing too hard for Him!

> *Ah, Sovereign* Lord, *you have made the heavens and the earth by your great power and outstretched arm. Nothing is too hard for you.* (Jer. 32:17)

Whatever great things God has done in the past, there is still more!

Good leaders are pioneers. They continually search for new opportunities to do what has never before been done. They are not content merely to maintain the status quo. Peter Drucker said, "Results are obtained by exploiting opportunities, not by solving problems. All one can hope to get by solving problems is to restore normalcy." Neither do leaders wait for circumstances to lead them in change, but they are initiators of change. They are not thermometers but thermostats! They do not follow where the path may lead; they go instead where there is no path and leave a trail.

Furthermore, they desire significant change. They seek God's face for His best. They want to turn around a dying church or failing business, or start up some new radical ministry or entrepreneurial venture, or revolutionize an existing process. They want to mobilize others in the face of strong inertia or resistance. They may not change the world, but they passionately pursue making a significant difference.

Moreover, leaders see the great potential that God has placed in their constituents – their gifts, talents and callings. Everywhere they look, leaders see divine opportunities and potentials.

Consider these visionary statements from Jesus and other New Testament leaders:

> *that all of them may be one, Father, just as you are in me and I am in you. May they also be in us so that the world may believe that you have sent me. I have given them the glory that you gave me, that they may be one as we are one: (John 17:21-22)*

> *And this gospel of the kingdom will be preached in the whole world as a testimony to all nations, and then the end will come. (Matt. 24:14)*

> *I pray that out of his glorious riches he may strengthen you with power through his Spirit in your inner being, so that Christ may dwell in your hearts through faith. And I pray that you, being rooted and established in love, may have power, together with all the saints, to grasp how wide and long and high and deep is the love of Christ, and to know this love that surpasses knowledge – that you may be filled to the measure of all the fullness of God. (Eph. 3:16-19)*

> *to prepare God's people for works of service, so that the body of Christ may be built up until we all reach unity in the faith and in the knowledge of the Son of God and become mature, attaining to the whole measure of the fullness of Christ… Instead, speaking the truth in love, we will in all things grow up into him who is the Head, that is, Christ. From him the whole body, joined and held together by every supporting ligament, grows and builds itself up in love, as each part does its work. (Eph. 4:12-15)*

> *But you are a chosen people, a royal priesthood, a holy nation, a people belonging to God, that you may declare the praises of him who called you out of darkness into his wonderful light. (1 Pet. 2:9)*

> *We proclaim to you what we have seen and heard, so that you also may have fellowship with us. And our fellowship is with the Father and with his Son, Jesus Christ. (1 John 1:3)*

Certainly these are all prophetic and doctrinal statements – as people usually interpret them – but they are primarily statements of *vision!* God is the ultimate Visionary! He is the ultimate Change Agent! This is why the Scriptures are filled with leadership vision from start to finish.

> *...the God who gives life to the dead and calls things that are not as though they were. (Rom. 4:17)*

Thus, leaders are not content merely to scrape through. Leaders want to transform; they are not content merely to maintain. This is one of the primary differences between leaders and spiritual managers. Leaders lead. They go first. They begin the quest for a new order. They plunge into new, sometimes dangerous, and always unpredictable territory. They take us to places we've never been before, and probably could never find on our own. Managers, on the other hand, maintain the existing order. They organize, and establish necessary processes and controls.

When a leader begins to seek new opportunities, he will, many times, not yet have a clear vision of what the future could be. That will come later. At first, he will usually have a sense of challenge and opportunity with an accompanying excitement and energy, but he may not be able to precisely define it. He will likely see some of the broad strategic details, but certainly not all of the technical details. Therefore, he must be comfortable with uncertainty and ambiguity, and be able to define and redefine as things move ahead.[4] This is why managers often accuse leaders of "flying by the seat of their pants"!

---

[4] This will help to locate you on the manager-leader continuum: how comfortable are you with uncertainty? Are you able to move ahead when you don't really know where you are going yet? For more on this distinction between leaders and managers, please see *Leaders & Managers: SpiritBuilt Leadership #5* by Malcolm Webber.

Moreover, the leader's vision will generally evolve in interaction with the people as well as the external context of the organization. Good visions are dynamic; they will change – and the new vision is usually better than the previous one!

Exemplary Leaders Challenge the Status Quo

As agents of change, leaders will:

- Pray and dream. This comes first. We must seek God's highest. In the Early Church, the leaders saw the central importance of this:

    In those days when the number of disciples was increasing, the Grecian Jews among them complained against the Hebraic Jews because their widows were being overlooked in the daily distribution of food. So the Twelve gathered all the disciples together and said, "It would not be right for us to neglect the ministry of the word of God in order to wait on tables. Brothers, choose seven men from among you who are known to be full of the Spirit and wisdom. We will turn this responsibility over to them and will give our attention to prayer and the ministry of the word." (Acts 6:1-4)

    Of course they had learned this from Jesus, who spent much time in the presence of His Father.

    Moreover, in Acts 13:1-3, the new vision of the apostolic ministry of Paul and Barnabas was birthed in an extended time of seeking God.

    While they were worshiping the Lord and fasting, the Holy Spirit said, "Set apart for me Barnabas and Saul for the work to which I have called them." (Acts 13:2)

Praying and dreaming take time. Consequently we must learn to graciously excuse ourselves from time-wasting busyness. We must learn to say, "No."

Effective leaders must be careful to not be so overwhelmed by today's problems that they lose sight of tomorrow's opportunities.

Jesus told His disciples to take time off to refresh their relationship with God before they burned out with their ministry responsibilities (Mark 6:30-32):

> *Then, because so many people were coming and going that they did not even have a chance to eat, he said to them, "Come with me by yourselves to a quiet place and get some rest." So they went away by themselves in a boat to a solitary place. (Mark 6:31-32)*

The outward effectiveness of our leadership will never exceed the quality of our inner life in God.

- Submit to God. To be effective, the leader's vision must come from God. Apart from Him we can accomplish nothing of any value:

  > *Remain in me, and I will remain in you. No branch can bear fruit by itself; it must remain in the vine. Neither can you bear fruit unless you remain in me. I am the vine; you are the branches. If a man remains in me and I in him, he will bear much fruit; apart from me you can do nothing. (John 15:4-5)*

  Paul recognized that it was only when he trusted in God that he was strong as a leader:

  > *But he said to me, "My grace is sufficient for you, for my power is made perfect in weakness." Therefore I will boast*

> *all the more gladly about my weaknesses, so that Christ's power may rest on me. (2 Cor. 12:9)*

A true vision comes from God. Then it becomes the leader's own vision; something he can share passionately with others. Without the divine initiation, however, man's vision is mere human ambition and God will not breathe on it.

> *For in the multitude of dreams and many words there is also vanity. But fear God. (Eccl. 5:7)*

- Constantly seek higher ground. There is always some new way to improve any organization. God has mighty things for us, and as we will seek His face He will show us His vision:

  > … *"No eye has seen, no ear has heard, no mind has conceived what God has prepared for those who love him" – but God has revealed it to us by his Spirit. The Spirit searches all things, even the deep things of God. (1 Cor. 2:9-10)*

  Let's seek His highest!

- Treat every responsibility as an adventure in an unexplored wilderness. If leaders want to inspire the best in others, they must find or create opportunities for people to outdo themselves in exploring new ground and reaching difficult goals. Furthermore, they must make ministry or work responsibilities enjoyable and exciting. Researchers have found that appropriate humor can lead to valuable cohesion and bonding between team members.

- Look for talent. This must become a part of your everyday consciousness. Be on the lookout for talent all the time. Don't wait around until you have a specific need. Watch people. Pay attention to their words and actions. If they look promising, engage them. Make a social connection. Talk to them about their work and their aspirations in God. Find out about their competencies, their experiences, their histories. The talent and resources for excellence are already present; they need merely to be unlocked. God is building His church. He has already placed many gifts and abilities in the people around you (1 Cor. 12:7). Leaders see opportunity everywhere – especially in the people who are already with them. Unfortunately, too many leaders complain that they do not have any good people when they are surrounded by them on every side!

> *… what they already had was more than enough to do all the work. (Ex. 36:7)*

- Question the status quo, and kill the sacred cows. Obviously, some standard practices and policies are critical to the organization's success. But many are simply traditions. Effective leaders ruthlessly examine everything in their organizations. "The way we've always done it" is insufficient reason to continue doing something. Is there a better way to do it? Is there even a better thing to do in the first place? Why do it this way? Why do it at all? Jesus challenged the religious status quo of His time. Indeed, the Gospel itself is nothing but a challenge to the status quo of man's condition in sin and death.

Jesus, the greatest Leader of all, continually confronted the status quo. He confronted dead religion, sin, spiritual blindness and alienation from God. He was not interested in incremental improvement; He came announcing a whole new kingdom!

The apostle, prophet, evangelist, teacher and pastor should all be change agents who seek the highest for God's people.

- Harvest new ideas – both inside and outside the organization. Many times the people who have been doing something for years have conceived of new and better processes. But no one has ever asked them for their opinion! Good leaders are listeners.[5] Moreover, there is a great harvest-field of innovative ideas outside the doors of every organization. Good leaders are learners. They continually explore – even in unrelated and entirely dissimilar fields. Effective leaders do not have to come up with every new idea themselves; they will recognize and advance the good changes that others dream up or initiate. A good leader may not be smart enough to come up with the good idea himself, but at least he's smart enough to recognize a good idea when he sees one! However, don't simply jump on the band-wagon; examine and adapt the ideas of others for your own situation. Moreover, don't just take; freely give your own ideas to others. Promote an attitude of "Steal this idea!" Engage in healthy creative exchange with others as much possible.

- Find something that needs fixing. "If it ain't broke, don't fix it" often doesn't cut it for a true leader. It may work well, but can it work better? In any case, does it even need to be done in the first place? Naïveté can be a leader's best friend in a new assignment. His dumb questions are tolerated as he uncovers needed improvements; and his fresh, uninstitutionalized approach can yield the conceptual breakthrough necessary for quantum leaps in organizational effectiveness.

- Believe in their people. The people are not just problems to be overcome; they must not be seen as merely "takers" but as potential "givers." In reality, the people are gifts from God to the church or ministry; thus, confidence in them is faith in the God who gave them. A truly effective leader will often be known for believing in his people more than they believe in themselves. Good leaders see potential futures in others and challenge them to fulfill God's destiny. Insecure leaders, on the other hand, will frequently project their own lack of confi-

---

[5] For more on this, please see *Listening: SpiritBuilt Leadership #12* by Malcolm Webber.

dence onto their people. What a leader sees in his people is largely determined by who he is. His assumptions about the ability of his people to succeed are based on his perception of his own leadership capability.

- Assign their people wisely. Organizations frequently commit the error of assigning their best people to deal with problems. Creative leaders, on the other hand, assign their people to opportunities. Naturally, problems must be dealt with, but opportunities are the life-blood of our churches and ministries. Solving a problem contains and prevents damage, but seizing an opportunity produces growth and new life. Opportunities are our connections with the future.

- Renew their teams. Even the best teams get stale and need to be revived. After a while, the members all think according to the same patterns. Bringing new people on board adds fresh perspective and energy. Leaders also require their people to interact with others and to listen for new ideas.

- Lead their people in continual learning. We all need to keep adding to our resource and skill bases – through reading a book, taking a course, attending a seminar, subscribing to a journal. Good leaders, and those who follow them, are lifetime learners.

- Have lots of ideas. The way to have a good idea is to have lots of them. In other words, if you have many good ideas, you will eventually have one!

    Cast your bread upon the waters, for after many days you will find it again. (Eccl. 11:1)

- Look for opportunities to glorify God. Christian leaders, above all, should seek opportunities to glorify God and accomplish His purposes with excellence.

Since leaders are always pushing ahead into unchartered realms, they must be prepared to take intelligent, calculated risks.

Exemplary Leaders Take Risks

Australians call this "having a go" or "giving it a shot."

Since leaders are forever venturing into uncharted waters, they are, of necessity, risk-takers. They are willing to experiment. In their quest for the new and the better, leaders are open to ideas. Like Peter, they are willing to get out of the "boats" of their own comfort zones (Matt. 14:29). They are willing to listen to others, and to try untested approaches, accepting the risks of failure that accompany all experimentation.

Living things change. Without constant innovation, an organization will atrophy. Even the most cutting-edge organizations adopt practices that become traditions. These traditions impose ways of thinking that become constraints, making it impossible to solve new problems or to exploit new opportunities. The leader is the organization's primary change agent. Thus, it is his responsibility to identify these barriers and to lead his people in breaking free from self-imposed limitations or "ceilings."

This "beyond-the-boundaries" thinking always involves risk. Successful leaders frequently acknowledge they failed many times before they succeeded, and famous people are often reported as saying it took them years to become an overnight success. You will never succeed unless you are willing to fail – and to be willing to fail is to assume some risk. This doesn't necessarily mean "betting the farm." Prudent risk taking should be the norm. One of the significant differences between the leader and the bureaucrat is the leader's inclination to encourage others to step out into the unknown rather than play it safe, and to learn from the mistakes that are the inevitable price we pay for innovation, change and learning.

It is through failures[6] that we learn. Consequently, failures are good and good failures are better since we can learn more. Failure is a master teacher if it has a willing student. The best failure of all is one that happens fast – so we can profit from it and move on before we have invested too much in a losing strategy.

We learn early in life that failure invites rejection and ridicule; consequently this willingness to risk failure does not come easily to many people. Perhaps it was the fear of failure that was driving the servant in Jesus' parable of the talents who buried the assets his lord had entrusted to him (Matt. 25:14-30)? When asked why he didn't do anything with what he had, he replied that he was afraid that he might make some mistakes, so he decided to preserve what he had.

The fear of failure paralyzes leadership. Imagine a wide and deep chasm between two cliffs with rocks at the bottom and someone is telling you to jump! This is an environment that does not allow mistakes. On the other hand, imagine a narrow and shallow chasm with a deep pool of cool, clear water at the bottom and someone is telling you to jump! This is an environment that does allow mistakes – especially on a hot day!

A friend taught one of my sons to walk on his hands. The first thing he did was to have my son stand up on his hands and then fall forward as he caught him. After doing this several times, my son overcame his natural fear of falling forward. The fear of falling forward is the greatest inhibitor to people learning to walk on their hands (in case you were wondering). But after my son actually fell forward a couple of times he realized that "failing" was not that painful after all. This emboldened him to continue to learn the new skill. Thus, to teach people to walk on their hands – or to do anything radically different – you must first provide an environment that reduces the costs of failure. It is this way with leadership. The leader must reduce the costs of failure for his people. He must make it possible for them to make mistakes without being crippled by them.

Think of when you learned a new sport or began to play a musical

---

[6] We are referring to strategic failures and not moral ones!

instrument. Did you do it perfectly the first time? Of course not! You had to take a risk when you first started – the risk of failure. The willingness to take a risk and to embrace the possibility of failure are essential to effective leadership. Anytime you begin to lead in some major change (which is the heart of leadership – helping people move from where they are to somewhere better), you will probably meet with resistance and things will probably go wrong – at least at first. You must persevere anyway! Risk and the possibility of failure are persistent elements of leadership.

A teacher of ballet was once asked about her young ballerinas, "Could you ever tell when a young girl would become a prima ballerina?" The teacher responded that while all the girls were limber and very flexible when young, the prima ballerinas were the ones who were willing to make fools of themselves. This is also the mark of a good leader: he is willing to take a risk and try something new.

As lifelong learners and risk-takers, leaders will:

- Set up little experiments. Leaders experiment with new approaches to old problems, and it is cheaper to do this in the early stages of innovation. When you have a new idea for a new ministry or approach, try it out soon. Don't wait until you've perfected it. On the other hand, don't bet the farm on a new idea.

- Make it safe for others to experiment. The leader sets the tone for the organization's creative climate. If the leader demands perfection and allows no mistakes, he will stifle vision. If you expect those you lead to venture out and take chances, you must make them feel safe and secure in doing so. As much as possible, reduce the costs of failure. Invite innovation and provide the resources necessary to nourish and sustain it. Furthermore, leaders encourage others to take risks by doing so themselves. They set the example and show the way.

- Stop the negativity. It is very easy to belittle new ideas. "If it ain't broke, don't fix it" is the mantra of those who cling to familiar territory. "It's too hard." "It'll never work." "We've never done it this way before." Like firefighters pouring water on a fire, these people douse innovation and extinguish enthusiasm. Leaders must discourage this draining negativity, and help people to see the possibilities that change brings. Members of one organization agreed that anyone heard firehosing should be required to contribute 25 cents to a fund. Team members then policed each other on a daily basis, morale improved noticeably, and so did the number of innovative ideas!

- Work even with ideas that sound strange initially. The lifeblood of any organization is a continual flow of new inspiration from God. Innovations rarely appear fully created and ready to implement; they usually require nurturing. Give every idea at least a chance. If you are too quick to reject new ideas, you will lose good ideas in the process and you will also discourage people from offering future ideas through fear of rejection. People who know that their ideas will receive a considered and balanced evaluation will be more likely to continue submitting ideas.

- Honor risk-takers. This boosts morale and reminds people of the need to take risks. Moreover, good attempts must be rewarded, not just successes.

- Debrief every failure as well as every success. Most innovations fail. Although it is tempting to let painful memories slide, the lessons are too valuable to be ignored. Especially learn from the failures of others – those are the cheapest mistakes! Ask the following questions: What did we do well? What did we do poorly? What did we learn from this? How can we do it better the next time?

- Rely on God. Pray that God will lead you to new paths of opportunity to fulfill His purposes. He is the greatest Innovator of all!

The Three Horizons

The effective church or Christian ministry will focus on three time horizons simultaneously:

1. Taking care of current responsibilities, extending and defending the core existing ministries.

    For example, a local church will have existing ministries relating to pastoral care, children, Sunday morning meetings, etc.

2. Building emerging ideas, strategies and processes. These are budding ministries that are not yet running at full speed. These initiatives need attention to build them up to be effective and fruitful. Some of these will become core processes in the future – especially when some of the old core ministries are fulfilled or lose their focus.

    For example, a local church may have begun a new small group strategy that is just starting to become effective.

3. Planting seeds for tomorrow. Healthy organizations encourage creativity and innovation for the long term. Not all of these seeds will bring forth an abundant harvest so a variety of initiatives need to be carried forward together. We must listen to the Holy Spirit – He knows everything about the future!

    For example, a local church may be praying and learning about how to send out missionaries in the future.

This pattern encompasses the mature, emergent and embryonic phases of an organization's life cycle. The leader is responsible to see that they are all addressed effectively. If any one of them is ignored there will be problems. If the current, core responsibilities are neglected then there will be no tomorrow. But if the future horizons are neglected, sooner or later the organization will become irrelevant.

Moreover, the top leader must ensure that the right people focus on the right horizons. The gifts and callings required to manage current responsibilities, to develop new strategies and to search out viable future directions are widely different from one another:

1. Taking care of present responsibilities (the first horizon) requires effective managers.

2. Developing emerging strategies (the second horizon) require builders – the typical "entrepreneurs" or leader-managers who can realistically connect long-range vision with the necessary daily realities of the organization.

3. The identification and creation of viable future opportunities (the third horizon) requires lateral thinkers and visionaries.

How to Improve

The following are some practical ways that you can improve in this area of leadership:

- Make a list of every task you are responsible for. About each one, ask yourself, "Why am I doing it this way? Why am I doing this at all? Can this task be done better? Does it need to be done at all? Should someone else be doing it?"

- Regularly ask your leaders, "What specific action did you take last week to improve your effectiveness this week?" When you ask, be ready to give your own answer to this same question. Do this several weeks in a row so they know you are serious about it.

- When you have leadership meetings, devote significant time (at least 25%) to improving processes and developing new ideas. In addition, spend significant time waiting on God for Him to reveal His vision (Acts 13:2).

- Ask your people what really annoys them about the organization. Change the most frequently mentioned items that hinder effectiveness. Be sure to fix any processes that are identified as broken. Also, stop doing anything that is identified as being unnecessary.

- Cultivate a positive attitude toward your people. Intentionally look for the good things in them, the potentials.

- Look for ideas. Visit churches or ministries that are effective in the specific areas you are weak in.

- Try something new. Do it on a small scale first, learn from it, then try again.

- Reward those who take risks. Affirm them publicly. Give them the opportunity to talk about their experiences and share what they have learned.

- Read biographies about God's "revolutionaries" – those who challenged the status quo and birthed great new things. Learn from them.

- Review your own vision. Identify "three horizons" in your own ministry. Please be specific.

BIBLICAL EXERCISES

1. Find examples in both testaments of leaders who challenged the status quo.

2. Find examples in both testaments of leaders who took intelligent risks.

chapter 3

Leaders Share the Vision

As we have seen, the leader defines the vision. However, that is not enough by itself. It is not enough just to have a high purpose. The leader must then share that purpose with the people he wants to follow him.

God's plan is for a united people to fulfill His purpose, not just for individual, gifted leaders to do great things.

Spiritual leaders must share their vision. There is a double meaning here to the word "share." Effective leaders communicate (share) the vision in such a way that their constituents personally embrace (share) it.

Before the leader can expect the people to follow he must ensure they are properly *aligned* with the vision. This means that they understand it and personally own it. Visionary leaders often make the mistake of trying to jump from establishing the vision to moving on the vision. But the second stage of bringing alignment must not be neglected or rushed.

The primary tool of alignment is communication. To be effective the vision must be communicated with clarity, passion and credibility. Clarity so the people know where to go; passion so they want to go; and credibility so they are willing to follow a leader they trust.

Without a clear and compelling vision you will not be able to lead anyone anywhere. Leaders capture the hearts of their followers with a passionate vision.

Consider how Jesus shared the Great Commission:

> Then Jesus came to them and said, "All authority in heaven and on earth has been given to me. Therefore go and make disciples of all nations, baptizing them in the name of the Father and of the Son and of the Holy Spirit, and teaching them to obey everything I have commanded you. And surely I am with you always, to the very end of the age." (Matt. 28:18-19)

It was not particularly detailed[7] but it was clear and simple. What would have been the result if Jesus had said, "Now I have no idea what happens next. I don't know what you're all going to do. Why don't you form a few small groups and discuss it, and let's see what you come up with?" Jesus was the Leader and He shared a vision that was passionate and clear.

Thus, leaders envision and share the future. Leaders can see what others have not yet seen. Leaders see beyond the normal, the ordinary, the expected. They gaze across time and imagine the greater things that can lie ahead. In doing so, they break through whatever limitations are holding the people back.

Leaders Break through Ceilings

Leaders who do not envision future opportunity for their people, instead of breaking through limitations, can actually establish limitations in the hearts and lives of their followers. Then those people can adopt those limitations as their own, and they can become self-imposed limitations (or ceilings) the people have for the rest of their lives.

Elephants have great memories but they aren't very smart. When they are babies their trainers can stake them down. The baby elephants try to tug away from the stake perhaps hundreds of times before they realize that they can't possibly get away. At that point, their "elephant memory" takes over and they remember for the rest of their lives that they can't get away from the stake. A limitation has been established in their lives. At

---

[7] In Acts 1:8, Jesus gives more broad strategic information – "Jerusalem, and in all Judea and Samaria, and to the ends of the earth" – but it is still not detailed.

this point, the strong stake can be replaced with a smaller wooden one, even though it wouldn't have enough strength to hold the elephant. An elephant trained in its babyhood to believe that the stake is strong and won't budge will not attempt to break loose and run away – even after it has grown strong enough to easily yank almost any stake out of the ground. In the same way, many people are limited for the rest of their lives by the negative words – from parents, teachers or spiritual leaders – and experiences of the past that have become ceilings preventing them from rising and fulfilling God's highest purposes.

Good leaders are ceiling busters! Vision is about possibility, and not probability. Probability involves merely the maintenance of the status quo. Leadership is about going somewhere else. Probabilities will likely happen if the present merely continues into the future, whereas possibilities need not be. But to a visionary leader, who imagines beyond the limitations and constraints that intimidate the hearts and minds of most, anything is possible! Effective leaders look beyond the expected into the realm of possibility. They look beyond the normal into the supernatural realm of God.

All new ventures begin with possibility thinking; and the clarity and force of this vision will sustain the leader through the rejection, failure and disappointment that inevitably accompany any truly new initiative. A leader's God-breathed vision acts as an organization's magnetic north. It attracts human energy. It invites and draws others to participate sacrificially in the divine mission. The leader's vision is what focuses the energy of the organization. Leaders see the possibilities of the future and then they share this vision with those they lead. Visions are conceptualizations, but they become real as leaders express them in concrete terms. Just as architects make drawings and engineers build models, leaders find ways of expressing their hopes for the future. Then the vision becomes like a lens that focuses unrefracted rays of light. The clearer the vision, the more compelling it is to all who follow. No matter how much involvement other people have in shaping the vision, the leader must be able to articulate it clearly. He must keep the vision focused. To help them in internally clarifying, and then externally expressing their vision, leaders should:

- Determine the will of God. God has very specific purposes for our lives and ministries. What are they? Unless our vision is based in the will and purpose of God, it will come to nothing. "Without Me you can do nothing" (John 15:5). "All our righteous acts are like filthy rags" (Isaiah 64:6). His vision must become our vision.

- Think about the past. Reflecting on our past enhances our ability to be forward thinking. As we contemplate the events of our lives – both the mountains and the valleys – we can identify our strengths and weaknesses, and the paradigms, patterns and themes that have carried us to the present, and which form the foundation on which our futures will be built.

- Test assumptions. Our assumptions often blind us to new solutions and opportunities. We should ask God to help us "think outside the box."

Consider the difference between "vertical" and "lateral" or "horizontal" thinking. Vertical thinking begins with a single concept and then proceeds with that concept until a solution is reached. Horizontal thinking refers to thinking that generates alternative ways of seeing a problem before seeking a solution. Vertical and horizontal thinking are like two different ways of digging holes. Logic is the tool that is used to dig holes deeper and bigger, to make them altogether better holes. But if the hole is in the wrong place, then no amount of improvement is going to put it in the right place. No matter how obvious this may seem to every digger, it is still easier to go on digging in the same place than to start all over again in a new place. In short, vertical thinking is digging the same hole deeper; horizontal thinking is trying again elsewhere. Certainly there appear to be some advantages in digging in the same hole since a half-dug hole offers a clear direction in which to expend effort. In addition, no one is paid to sit around being capable of achievement. As there is no way of assessing such capability it is necessary to pay and promote according to visible achievements. Far better to dig the wrong hole (even one that is recognized as being wrong) to an impressive depth than to sit around wondering where to start digging. However, many holes are being dug to an impractical depth, many in the wrong place, and breakthroughs usually result from someone abandoning a partly-dug hole and beginning anew in a different place.

- Follow the inward leading of the Holy Spirit. Visions in their early stages can be somewhat vague and ill-defined. It may take time to shape a new vision to the point of lucid articulation. So, instead of struggling with words on paper, we should do something to act on our inward leading or intuition. Visions, like objects in the distance, become clearer as we move toward them.

- Write a short vision statement. A compelling vision must be shared in a few words. Vision statements should capture the essential purpose and nature of the new initiative. Moreover, the vision statement must be clear and passionate. The clearer and more passionate the vision, the greater the fire it will ignite, and the easier it will be to develop the strategy to achieve it.

The vision will provide a "strategic umbrella" in the sense that it will describe a clear strategic direction in overarching terms for the organization. The general nature of the overarching goals of the vision will allow for more specific, tactical goals to be formulated as opportunities arise and barriers appear. The vision will provide broad action guidelines.

A well-articulated vision provides the people at all levels in the organization with a simple memory tool to align their values, actions, and decisions with the organization's strategic objectives. Its simplicity also promotes clarity of focus. Through minimization of the number of goals, organizational resources are more likely to be focused.

- Live in the future. The Holy Spirit is Lord of the future as well as of the past and present. We should ask Him what the future holds for our churches and ministries. Whose view of the future is dominating our lives, our organizations and our strategies? Is it God's?

Leaders Enlist Others

It is not enough for the leader to have a grand vision; his followers must "buy into" his dream.

You may have the highest purpose in the world, but if you don't share that vision with your constituents, and do it in such a way that it captures their hearts, they will not follow you.

When properly communicated, a divinely-inspired vision will empower positive change by focusing the collective energy of all involved, and by building commitment and a willingness to take personal responsibility for the organization's success. "A million candles can be lit from a single flame."

The servant-heart of the godly leader desires to transform the lives of his constituents. He is not interested in people merely going through the motions of following his vision. He wants them to genuinely share the vision. Consequently, he seeks to capture their hearts with the vision. He avoids the temptation to use coercion, reward or positional power to get the people to follow.

Sometimes Christian leaders have good goals, but they try to mandate those goals for their followers. They become authoritarian and demanding, and try to force the people to move toward those goals by brute force. For example, they may try to manipulate the people through guilt, fear, or some form of bribe.

Good leaders, however, envision their constituents. They capture their hearts with a vision of the possibilities of God in their lives. They share a vision that fires the imagination, builds a sense of dedication, and motivates into action.

The leader must give the people a high vision. Not a foolish vision; it should be attainable. It should be realistic and not just be "big talk." But it should be high. If the people aren't called to a big vision, they will respond with little commitment. A little vision attracts little commitment. A big vision attracts big commitment. High causes attract high dedication.

Some leaders look longingly at other churches or ministries where the people are accomplishing a lot, and wish that they had people that were as spiritual. In reality, it is a leadership problem, not a people problem.

So often, we set the bar too low. We need to raise the bar. We should not do it in a demanding or coercive way. But we should challenge the people. We should share a vision that we believe they are capable of, and we should tell them that, and then encourage them in various ways to go for it. That's what attracts big dedication – a big vision; an audacious vision.[8]

If we set a vision of mediocrity before our followers, what do we expect them to do? By our own unbelief, by our own lack of vision, we have actually established a ceiling over our people. We have established limitations on their lives that they may never break through.

Good leaders punch through the ceilings. They don't let a ceiling be an obstruction; they make it a target!

We must raise expectations. Our people will achieve a lot more in God, if we will raise the bar – if we will raise the vision. We must break out of the bounds of the present and the past, and look into the limitless future. God holds the future; the future is not bound.

---

[8] Many religious cults understand this. They capture the hearts of people with a very high call for commitment. Sadly, too many churches do not.

Leaders Share the Vision

Even the most "on-fire" leaders cannot accomplish extraordinary things alone. Neither is this God's purpose. He wants an army of ordinary people to do His will, not just spiritual superstars.

To enlist others to rally around a common vision, leaders will:

- Identify their constituents. Leaders must first identify all those who have a stake in the outcome of what they envision. This will include all the members of their church or ministry, other leaders, and even members of the community. Broad visions need broad support to be accomplished.

- Appeal to a common purpose. No matter how grand the vision is, if people don't see in it the possibility of realizing their own hopes and dreams, they won't follow. By knowing their constituents, leaders are able to fuse them together around a common purpose.

If they are to embrace it, the vision must be genuinely meaningful to the people. When the people perceive that their leader's vision is meant to serve them rather than just serve the leader, the following occurs:

1. They will permit the leader to deviate from certain organizational norms and traditions.
2. They will have a greater tolerance of whatever personality quirks the leader may have.
3. They will be more willing to suspend their judgment of innovative or risky proposals advocated by the leader.
4. Failures are not likely to be evaluated as harshly.
5. The leader will have the credibility necessary to garner the people's commitment to the vision and to the hard work it will take to achieve it.

Often, the people are not as wedded to the status quo as their leaders think they are. Many times, people are waiting on their leaders!

- Listen first – and often. Listening is one of the key characteristics of exemplary leaders. By taking time to listen, leaders can hear what their constituents want included in the vision, and thus build a truly shared destiny. This process is not a monologue but a dialogue. An effective leader does not merely impose his own personal dream, but he develops a shared sense of purpose.

There is a balance between the top leader establishing the direction for the organization and the people participating in that process. Here is how the process works. The top leader establishes the general direction for the people in accordance with the Word of God and the leading of the Holy Spirit. But then each subgroup within the church or ministry is free to develop more specific focus within, and aligned with, the overall broad vision. The initial broad vision for the organization is essentially unilateral; there is minimal dialogue. The dialogue increases as the scope is narrowed to individual ministries, and individuals within those ministries. Individual leaders within the organization should dialogue with the primary vision carrier as they define their own specific place and purpose.

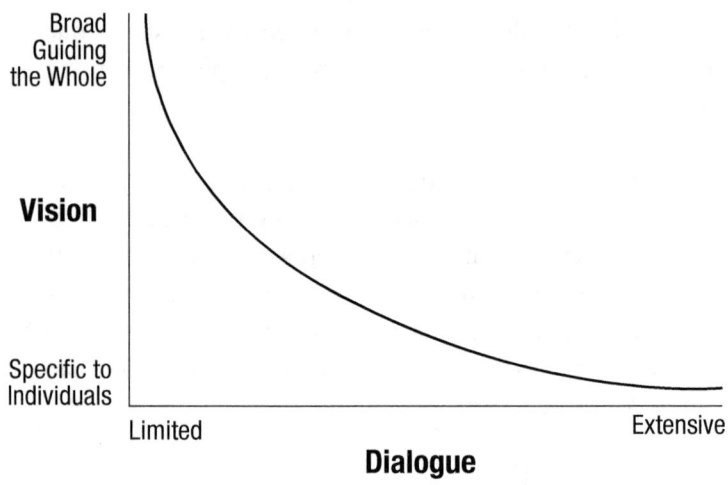

The degree to which the establishment of the vision is a dialogue is relative to the broadness of the vision as well as to the following:

- The top leader's personal involvement in the carrying out of the agenda. As this decreases, the vision should become more of a dialogue. The people who actually do it should define it and refine it.

- Fineness of detail. As this increases, the vision becomes more a dialogue. The top leader will not be in touch with all the necessary details of what goes on.

- Scope of possibilities. As these increase, dialogue should increase.

- Breathe life into the vision. By using vivid metaphors, stories, symbols and slogans, and by communicating with fire and enthusiasm, leaders make their intangible vision come alive so that others can see it, hear it, taste it and touch it.

- Speak positively. There is no room for tentativeness when

we share the vision. The obstacles and difficulties should be addressed, but not dwelled on. Leaders must express to their followers that, together, they are well able to succeed and to "take the land"!

- To be effective, vision must be shared with clarity, passion and credibility. Clarity so the people know where to go; passion so they want go; and credibility so they are willing to follow a leader they trust.

- Speak from the heart. The greatest inhibitor to enlisting others in a common vision is a lack of personal conviction. Others will never share a dream if the leader is not fully convinced of it himself. Leaders must genuinely believe in their own dream; then the vision will live and compel. Moreover, leaders must believe in the future of their followers. If the leader does not believe in it, how can he convince them to? The leader must believe his own vision and it will become alive as he shares it with his people. According to C.T. Studd a leader must be able to speak with seven times the passion he wants the people to possess. They may not be clear about all the technical details, but leaders' hearts should beat with a passionate vision.

How to Improve

The following are some practical ways that you can improve in this area of leadership:

- Find out what reputable people are predicting will happen in the next ten years. How will your church or ministry be affected?

- Define where you are going in your life. Formulate a personal vision statement, by contemplating the following questions:

- What does God want me to accomplish?
- If there were absolutely no limits on me, what would I choose to do?
- What is my dream?
- What obsesses me?
- How do I want to impact the world?
- About what do I have a burning passion?

- Talk to some of your key constituents and ask them about their hopes, dreams, and goals for the future. How do these relate to your own? How can you incorporate their godly aspirations into yours?

- Ask your constituents to share their dreams and aspirations with one another. Ask them to listen carefully and to identify common goals. Make these common goals visible to all.

- What are the present ceilings or limitations in your life and ministry? Identify them and form a plan for punching through them. Encourage your constituents to do the same.

- Write a five minute "vision speech" for your organization, based upon what you imagine you will have achieved in five to ten years time. Use symbols and imagery in this speech. Strive for passion and clarity.

- Talk constantly about the future with everyone you meet.

- Expose yourself to the writings, speeches and life stories of Christian visionaries, especially the great communicators among them. Watch them if possible in person or by video. Learn from them.

BIBLICAL EXERCISES

1. Find examples in both testaments of leaders whose visions broke through ceilings for themselves and others.

2. Find examples in both testaments of leaders who shared their visions effectively with others.

chapter 4

Leaders Shift the Vision

Having first conceived the vision, the leader must now shift the vision to those who will actually be responsible for bringing it to pass. This process began when the leader shared the vision with the people. Now he must accomplish "vision-shift." He must actually give away the capacity to fulfill the vision. He must build a team that will act on the vision and bring it to pass.

According to the New Testament, the role of the leader is not merely to do the ministry but to equip the people to minister.

> *It was he who gave some to be apostles, some to be prophets, some to be evangelists, and some to be pastors and teachers, to prepare God's people for works of service, so that the body of Christ may be built up... From him the whole body, joined and held together by every supporting ligament, grows and builds itself up in love, as each part does its work. (Eph. 4:11-16)*

For many spiritual leaders this is a radical shift in mindset: to become a team-builder instead of being someone who just does it all himself – to move from focusing on the task to focusing on the people.

Collaboration

Effective leaders strengthen others and foster collaboration. Nothing truly great occurs without the active involvement and support of many people. Fulfilling the purpose of God for our organizations must be everyone's responsibility, and good leaders promote teamwork rather than competition as the road to success. Competition (which is trying to beat others) is vastly different in purpose from collaboration (which is trying to do well together). Competition is the old paradigm; collaboration is the new.

The relationships of the team members are the organization's key assets, and leaders must know how to nurture them. In building a strong team out of people with diverse and sometimes conflicting interests, leaders must develop cooperative goals, seek integrative solutions and build trusting relationships, through:

- Always saying "we." The leader's task is to help people reach mutual goals and not merely his own goals. Inclusive language will communicate the fact that goals are truly collaborative and not exploitative. This will lead to stable and committed relationships that are able to weather conflicts and difficulties.

- Building the team with the right people. A wise leader will populate his team according to his own weaknesses. Some leaders make the mistake of staffing their team with people who are just like themselves. The effective leader will surround himself with people whose strengths make up for his own weaknesses, as well as bringing people on board who share his own strengths. When Jesus built His leadership team for the future, He brought together a very diverse group of people whose strengths and weaknesses balanced each other.

- Sustaining ongoing interactions between team members. The leader must ensure that team members do not work in isolation from one another. Formal and informal meetings will help, as will sharing resources. Teams should be limited in size to a "knowable" number of people. For example, Jesus' top leadership team consisted of 12 men. Moreover, team members must be encouraged to work through their conflicts together rather than using the leader as a go-between. Like Paul in Philippians 4:2, the leader must refuse to "take sides" but maintain his equal commitment to all team members.

- Focusing on gains, not losses. When dealing with problems, team members must be led to focus on their areas of agreement first, rather than their differences. Deliberately recognizing the alignment of everyone's goals is a powerful way to create a sense of mutuality. Furthermore, emphasizing the long-term nature of the team's goals will strengthen the vision and assist collaboration.

- Viewing differences[9] as creative opportunities, and not as threats.[10] In reality, differences can generate more alternatives – and thus new opportunities – than similarities do. The leader must ask lots of questions and listen closely to the needs, problems and ideas of the team members, to find solutions no one has previously discovered.

---

[9] We have strategic and personality differences in view here – not doctrinal differences or ethical standards!

[10] Irving Janis, a Yale social psychologist, defined *groupthink* as "a mode of thinking that people engage in when they are deeply involved in a cohesive in-group, when the members' strivings for unanimity override their motivation to realistically appraise alternative courses of action." Groupthink requires that members share a strong "we-feeling" of solidarity and desire to maintain cohesive relationships within the group at all costs. When colleagues operate in a groupthink mode, they automatically apply the "preserve group harmony" test to every decision they face. This "superglue" of solidarity can increase a team's effectiveness and unity; however, it also often causes their mental process to get stuck and militates against critical and creative thinking.

- Trusting team members. People who cannot trust others, fail to become effective leaders. Often they also burn out. They end up either doing all the work themselves or supervising it so closely they become overbearing and controlling. Moreover, their demonstration of lack of trust for others undermines others' trust in them.

- To build strong partnerships, leaders should involve the people closest to the work in planning and solving problems associated with it. They are the most qualified to make those decisions anyway. Delegation builds broad ownership and establishes an atmosphere of trust.

- Going first. One cannot legislate true cooperation or trust. As the leader first shows a willingness to cooperate and to trust others, his example encourages others to do the same. Thus, leaders should be open and honest with others regarding their own limitations and mistakes, and should be liberal with information, resources, spontaneous (versus mechanical) affirmations, showing genuine interest, and giving a listening ear. They should also avoid talking negatively about other team members. They must not allow themselves to be pulled into camps, but instead be "camp busters"!

- Simplifying structure. Instead of a complicated bureaucratic structure in your team, work on developing a simpler structure that makes decision-making and communication easier,[11] and is capable of rapid growth.

- Listening to the Holy Spirit. We must allow the Holy Spirit to crucify our natural competitiveness, and to replace it with the

---

[11] A good exercise that demonstrates the ineffectiveness of communication in a complex bureaucratic structure is as follows. Share a complicated message quietly with the first person in a group and have him whisper it to the person next to him and so forth around the whole group. Then compare the final version with the original – the results will usually be quite humorous!

servant attitude of Jesus. Moreover, He will show us the true nature of our churches and ministries, exposing what needs to be changed, and helping us to build effective teams that will accomplish His purposes and bring Him glory.

Power Generators

In organizations that rely on external power and control to make people perform, the constituents rarely achieve their best. The capacity of individuals and organizations to excel grows when the people do things because they want to, and not because they have to. When people are mere powerless pawns, they feel weak and insignificant. Empowered people, however, possess greater confidence, determination and effectiveness. Exemplary leaders accomplish great things by enabling others to take ownership of and responsibility for the organization's success.

As the following chart demonstrates, when you give away responsibility you must also give away authority.

What Is Empowerment?

$$E = R + A + E^2$$
Empowerment = Responsibility + Authority + lots of Encouragement

$$R - A = F^2$$
Responsibility without Authority produces much Frustration and Failure

$$E = O$$
Empowerment = Ownership

Leaders have a choice: they can hold onto their power (authority, responsibility and privilege) and use it purely for selfish ends, or they can give their power away to others. The more power you have, the less you should use, and the more you should give away.

Servant leaders who take the power that flows to them and connect it to others, become power generators from which their constituents draw strength. Jesus did this:

> *Then Jesus came to them and said, "All authority in heaven and on earth has been given to me. Therefore [you] go and make disciples of all nations..." (Matt. 28:18-19)*

The Great Commission marked a profound transition. Until this point, Jesus had been totally responsible for the work of the kingdom of God on the earth. Now He was turning this responsibility over to His team. Notice that He did not only give them responsibility, He also gave them *authority*.

> *I will give you the keys of the kingdom of heaven; whatever you bind on earth will be bound in heaven, and whatever you loose on earth will be loosed in heaven. (Matt. 16:19)*

> *If you forgive anyone his sins, they are forgiven; if you do not forgive them, they are not forgiven. (John 20:23)*

> *And these signs will accompany those who believe: In my name they will drive out demons... they will place their hands on sick people, and they will get well. (Mark 16:17-18)*

Clearly, Jesus was more capable than His disciples to do all of this, yet He gave power away. In addition to the Lord Jesus, there are many biblical examples of leaders who gave power away:

- God Himself gave power to Adam to care for the garden (Gen. 2:15), name the animals (Gen. 2:19), and rule over the world (Ps. 8:4-6). Clearly, God was more capable than Adam to do all of this, yet He gave power away.
- Moses returned from Mt. Sinai with the plans for the tabernacle, but then he gave away the responsibility for its actual building.
- Jethro advised Moses to give power away to "capable men" (Ex. 18:13-26).

- When the Levitical priesthood was established, there was a clear division of labor as well as a hierarchy of responsibility (Num. 18:1-4, especially v. 3a).
- Solomon delegated responsibility to those who managed his nation, armies, palace, provisions and taxes (1 Kings 4).
- The apostles gave power away to the seven in Acts 6.

Sharing Power with Others

The seven leadership essentials of sharing power with others are:

1. Give power away. Paradoxically, leaders become more powerful when they give their own power away. Leadership power is not a fixed and limited sum – like a pie that is divided into pieces – to be hoarded and grudgingly divided up only when absolutely necessary. Everyone benefits when a leader gives power away. No one loses – especially not the leader! A leader's power is not reduced when he empowers others. Organizationally, power actually consolidates and multiplies when it is shared with others. When people have responsibility and genuine influence, their commitment to the organization and its success drastically increases. The key to unleashing an organization's potential to excel is putting the power in the hands of the people who perform the work. Thus, leaders must trust and respect their constituents, and they must know their people well enough to empower them appropriately. Jesus is our ultimate Model for this (Matt. 10:1; Mark 16:15-20).

2. Facilitate decision-making authority. Good leaders will enlarge their constituents' spheres of influence, and will provide them with greater decision-making authority and responsibility. They will remove or reduce unnecessary approval steps, eliminate as many rules as possible, increase people's flexibility regarding processes, support the exercise of independent

judgment, encourage creative solutions to problems, define jobs more broadly (as projects, not tasks), provide the resources necessary for success, and support freedom of organizational communication (both vertically and horizontally).

3. Develop competence. If people are to succeed in their new and increasing responsibilities, they need to develop their capacities. Leaders must invest in developing their people's skills and competencies.

4. Assign critical tasks. Jesus did this in Matthew 28. People's increased sphere of influence ought to involve something relevant to the most pressing concerns and core issues of the organization. We do our best when our work is critical to success. Empowerment should be genuinely significant and not merely a token acquiescence to the latest management fad. Moreover, leaders should regularly inform their constituents regarding the organization's performance and the evolving challenges it faces.

5. Stretch them. When giving a new assignment to an emerging leader, determine what you think his capacities are. Then give him an assignment a little more than that.[12] Do not make it too high, or else he will fail and be discouraged. But if you make it beneath his capacities, he will also be discouraged by the lack of challenge. If you give him an assignment equal to his capacities he will soon master it and become bored. Go a little higher, and then let him surprise you! Because it is a challenge he will look to God for success and then rise to his full potential with God's help; the resulting success will strengthen his faith and establish his confidence in moving ahead into even greater challenges. This is how we help people grow – not by playing it safe, but by challenging them!

---

[12] Although do *not* give him responsibilities beyond his character (1 Tim. 3:6, 10; 5:22-25)!

Give Stretching Assignments!

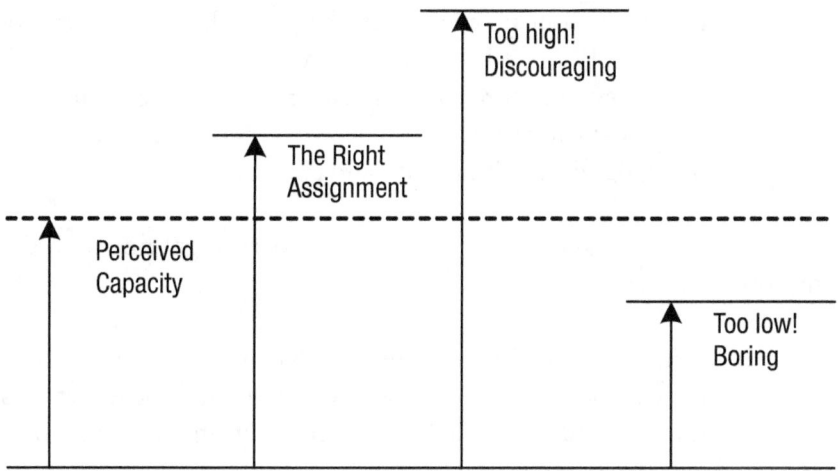

Your priority is not simply to get the task done, but to build the person for the future. So, don't play it safe!

Jesus gave His disciples challenging assignments even when they were not perfect. In Mark 16, Jesus gave them an extraordinary assignment immediately after they had failed three times (vv. 8, 11, 13-14)! Two thousand years later, almost 700 million believers around the world demonstrate the wisdom of Jesus' strategy here; it worked! Certainly, Jesus' disciples made some errors along the way, but in the long term it worked![13]

6. Offer visible support. It is who you know that counts. Leaders should assist their people in making connections and building strong relationships with others who can help them accomplish their tasks – both inside and outside the church or ministry. Facilitating this networking is empowering. Also, by making visible heroes and heroines of others, a leader will increase those people's power as well as build a stronger bond between

---

[13] For more on stretching assignments, please see *Building Leaders: SpiritBuilt Leadership #4* by Malcolm Webber.

himself and them.

7. Believe in your people. Researchers call this the "Pygmalion Effect."[14] When a leader genuinely expects his people to do well, they will. Stretch those around you. Give them more than what you think they're capable of. Moreover, speak life to them, not death. Speak faith and encouragement!

The following are some of the reasons why leaders might find it hard to give power away:

1. Failure to plan. To simply recruit someone at the last moment to do something is "dumping," not delegating. The leader must think ahead, communicate thoroughly and commit to an effective ongoing oversight.

2. Pride. Of course, we all know that no one else could ever do the job as well as we can! However, the example of Jesus instructs us – *He* was not too proud to give power away! If Jesus could give power away, then we are not indispensable!

3. Lack of vision. If our vision is limited to our existing four walls, then we will see no need to expand the leadership base. However, if we have a vision for growth and impact, then we know that growth requires leader development and empowerment. Pyramids are made tall by widening their foundations. Spectators become critics; participants become partners.

---

[14] The theory behind the Pygmalion Effect is that people will act the way you treat them. In George Bernard Shaw's classic tale of "Pygmalion" (which later became the movie, "My Fair Lady") a sophisticated professor of phonetics bet his friend he could take a common flower girl and transform her into a lady. When Professor Higgins treated Eliza Doolittle like a lady, she began to believe she was a lady and behaved accordingly. In the Greek story from which Shaw drew his title, Pygmalion was a famous sculptor of the Greek island of Crete who made a statue of a beautiful woman. When he fell in love with the statue, his desire along with help from the gods caused the statue to become alive.

The benefits of giving power away are significant:

1. Everyone avoids burnout.

   > *Moses' father-in-law replied, "What you are doing is not good. You and these people who come to you will only wear yourselves out. The work is too heavy for you; you cannot handle it alone… select capable men from all the people – men who fear God, trustworthy men who hate dishonest gain – and appoint them as officials over thousands, hundreds, fifties and tens… That will make your load lighter, because they will share it with you. If you do this and God so commands, you will be able to stand the strain, and all these people will go home satisfied." (Ex. 18:17-23)*

2. Everyone can focus on what they're called to do and are actually good at.

   > *So the Twelve gathered all the disciples together and said, "It would not be right for us to neglect the ministry of the word of God in order to wait on tables. Brothers, choose seven men from among you who are known to be full of the Spirit and wisdom. We will turn this responsibility over to them and will give our attention to prayer and the ministry of the word." (Acts 6:2-4)*

   > *We have different gifts, according to the grace given us. If a man's gift is prophesying, let him use it in proportion to his faith. If it is serving, let him serve; if it is teaching, let him teach; if it is encouraging, let him encourage; if it is contributing to the needs of others, let him give generously; if it is leadership, let him govern diligently; if it is showing mercy, let him do it cheerfully. (Rom. 12:6-8)*

3. We will build leaders. This is one of the key ways in which leaders are built – through accepting responsibilities and "challenging assignments."

   He appointed twelve – designating them apostles – that they might be with him and that he might send them out to preach and to have authority to drive out demons. (Mark 3:14-15)

4. The ministry multiplies. As D.L. Moody said, "It's better to get ten men to do the work than to do the work of ten men!"

   Five of you will chase a hundred, and a hundred of you will chase ten thousand... (Lev. 26:8)

5. God has commanded us to give power away!

   It was he who gave some to be apostles, some to be prophets, some to be evangelists, and some to be pastors and teachers, to prepare God's people for works of service, so that the body of Christ may be built up until we all reach unity in the faith and in the knowledge of the Son of God and become mature, attaining to the whole measure of the fullness of Christ. (Eph. 4:11-13)

Necessary Organizational Changes

To fully empower their people, effective leaders will eliminate organizational conditions that foster a sense of powerlessness among the people. Some of these are:

- Organizational factors:
    - Impersonal bureaucratic climate.
    - Poor communication/network-forming systems.
    - Highly centralized organizational resources.

- Supervisory style:
  - Authoritarian (high control).
  - Negativism (emphasis on failures).
  - Lack of reason for actions/consequences.

- Reward system:
  - Arbitrary reward allocation.
  - Low incentive value of rewards.
  - Lack of competence-based rewards.
  - Lack of innovation-based rewards.

- Job/Responsibility Design:
  - Lack of role clarity.
  - Lack of training and technical support.
  - Unrealistic goals.
  - Lack of appropriate authority.
  - Low task variety.
  - Limited participation in programs, meetings, and decisions that have a direct impact on performance.
  - Lack of appropriate/necessary resources.
  - Lack of network-forming opportunities.
  - Highly established work routines.
  - High rule structure.
  - Low advancement opportunities.
  - Lack of meaningful goals/tasks.
  - Limited contact with senior leadership.

In genuinely empowering his people, the leader will avoid or eliminate such conditions in the organization.

How to Improve

The following are some practical ways that you can improve in this area of leadership:

- Look over the above list of conditions that foster a sense of powerlessness and determine which ones apply to your organization. Make specific plans to change these conditions.

- Find ways to increase interaction between people who need to work more effectively together. These ways should be both formal and informal.

- Commit to changing your vocabulary – use "we" instead of "I." In everything you communicate promote an inclusive sense of teamwork and sharing.

- Consider what important tasks you now have that you can assign to others. As you do so, coach and support them.

- Assign non-routine work to people who usually do routine work. This will increase their sense of power and ownership.

- Ask your coworkers for their opinions about things. Share problems with them.

- Ensure that everyone receives sufficient ministry-related training – at least 40 hours each year.

- Admit your mistakes and be honest when you don't know. Be willing to change your mind when someone comes up with a better idea.

- Remove unnecessary steps in approval processes.

- On a regular basis, share information with people about how well the church or ministry is doing, according to whatever measures are appropriate. When people know how things are going, they are more empowered.

- Give people a choice about being a part of a particular project. This will increase their commitment to it.

- Make it public when teams work well together. Exemplify what teamwork is all about.

- Instead of leading all the meetings yourself, ask different people to do so. In addition, practice being a facilitator instead of a manager at meetings.

- Choose someone in your organization who is known as an exceptional "people person." Watch them. Ask them for advice on how you can do better.

BIBLICAL EXERCISES

1. Find examples in both testaments of leaders who built effective teams that possessed a strong sense of personal ownership.

2. Find examples in both testaments of leaders who gave power away.

chapter 5

Leaders Show the Vision

Good leaders "show" or validate the vision to their constituents by doing two things:

1. They personally set the example and thus demonstrate how to fulfill the vision.
2. They plan small wins and thus demonstrate that the vision will work.

As they do this momentum is gained and the vision is moved along toward success.

Leaders Personally Set the Example

People learn the Christian life and Christian leadership through modeling:

> *… learn of me… (Matt. 11:29)*

> *I have set you an example that you should do as I have done for you. (John 13:15)*

> *Follow my example, as I follow the example of Christ. (1 Cor. 11:1)*

> *Join with others in following my example, brothers, and take note of those who live according to the pattern we gave you. (Phil. 3:17)*

> *Remember your leaders, who spoke the word of God to you. Consider the outcome of their way of life and imitate their faith. (Heb. 13:7; see also 1 Thess. 1:6; 2 Thess. 3:7-9; 1 Cor. 4:16; 1 Pet. 2:21-23; 1 Tim. 4:12; 2 Tim. 1:13; Tit. 2:7; Heb. 6:12)*

People need models; not just instructions. The following game demonstrates this quite dramatically. Have one person look at a letter in the Hebrew alphabet and describe this to someone else (who does not know Hebrew) so that the second person can draw it. This will take some time and be quite difficult. Afterwards, have the second person look at the letter and then draw it. This will be much easier, demonstrating the reality that people need models to follow, not only instructions.

In ancient times the word "example" came from the Greek word "a copy" (e.g., 1 Pet. 2:21). It referred to a pattern to write or paint by. Technically, this was a pattern given by writing-masters to their pupils, containing all the letters of the alphabet, to be traced over. The Greek word was also used of an architect drawing a building so that the builders could copy it.

It is not enough for us to deliver rousing speeches and to write visionary materials; leaders must actually participate in the doing of what they ask others to do. Leading by example is how leaders provide evidence that they are deeply and personally committed to the vision they champion. Credible leaders practice what they preach. They do what they say they will do, and thus become the model for others to follow. This establishes the integrity of the vision.

Exemplifying Values

Leaders set the example by behaving in ways that are consistent with their organization's shared values. They accomplish this by:

- Clarifying their own personal values. People expect their leaders to stand for something, and to have the courage of their convictions. Leaders who lack core values are likely to change their position with every fad, and will be judged eventually as inconsistent and "political" in their behavior (think of the common practice of politicians leading their countries according to the results of the polls – "the tail wagging the dog"). Values are the standards that help us determine what we will and will not do. They influence every aspect of our lives: our moral judgments, our responses to others, our commitments to personal and organizational goals. A Christian leader's values must be based directly upon the eternal Scriptures and not the latest opinion poll. People want to follow a leader with conviction.

- Building a consensus of shared values based upon the Scriptures. For the people to be mobilized in unity, they must all share the same values. Thus the leaders, through the clear teaching of Scripture, must gain consensus on a common cause and a common set of principles, thereby building a community of shared values that will form the solid bedrock of an organization's vitality and effectiveness. This takes time since the people must truly own the values; unity is forged, not forced. Biblical values are not negotiable but it still takes time for the people to understand and personally own them.

- Watching their own actions. People pay more attention to the values their leaders actually use than to those the leaders say they believe in (i.e. the official "values statement"). Effective leaders must set good examples, establish high standards for themselves, and personally practice what they preach. A profitable exercise in this regard is to list the values you preach and then systematically compare them with those values actually reflected by your calendar and checkbook for the last month. To be consistent, how you spend your time and money should line up with your espoused priorities.

> *In everything I did, I showed you that by this kind of hard work we must help the weak, remembering the words the Lord Jesus himself said: "It is more blessed to give than to receive." (Acts 20:35)*

This point highlights the serious responsibility of being a leader. In the end, the people will do what they see you teach *and* do.

- Seizing teachable moments. Critical incidents present opportunities for leaders to teach important lessons about appropriate norms of behavior. Effective leaders will watch for these opportunities, and use them to illuminate and reinforce the organization's values.

- Following in the footsteps of the Lord Jesus and His leaders. The call to imitate godly leaders as they walk in righteousness, and not only talk it, is found throughout the New Testament.

Small Wins

By planning small wins, leaders demonstrate that the vision will work. As the Chinese idiom declares, we must "win the first battle."

How do you eat an elephant? One bite at a time, of course! The most effective change processes are incremental. Leaders who try to accomplish the extraordinary must learn the discipline of breaking down big problems and opportunities into small, doable steps. Problems that are conceived of too broadly overwhelm us, but anybody can take "just one more step." Leaders help others to see how progress can be made by breaking the journey down into achievable goals and milestones. This makes the task more easily understood and accomplished.

> *But you will receive power when the Holy Spirit comes on you; and you will be my witnesses in Jerusalem, and in all Judea and Samaria, and to the ends of the earth. (Acts 1:8)*

Sometimes visionary leaders do not recognize that their followers are unable to understand or embrace the magnitude of their vision. If he doesn't break the vision down into understandable and achievable steps, such a leader will most likely lose his followers either through confusion or exhaustion.

Moreover, when only a small task is tackled, the chances of success are much higher, and the "small-wins" process enables leaders to build momentum and their constituents' commitment to the broader course of action. This creates a climate in which success is not only seen as possible, but imminent.

In leading the small-wins process and building commitment to the long-term vision, leaders will:

- Take it personally. If you're the leader, the first small-win "unit" is you. Actions speak louder than words and build your credibility. What new initiatives have you taken lately? What small battles have you won?

- Make a broad plan. You'll never be able to foresee it all, and by the time you get there it will likely all be different anyway. Nevertheless, you've got to start somewhere and the process of planning gets people to mentally walk through the entire journey, anticipating the events, milestones, tasks and goals, and imagining their success.

- Within the parameters of the overall vision, give people choices. Choice is the cement that binds action to the person, motivating individuals to take ownership and accept responsibility for what they do.

- Break it down. Once you've set your sights, move forward incrementally – especially at the beginning. Break large groups and goals into small cohesive teams and doable tasks. There is nothing more discouraging than starting off with a failure, so make sure you include a few early successes in your plan.

- Publicize your commitments and your progress. By making your corporate goals visible, you create accountability and increase everyone's sense of obligation to the vision. Then by publicizing successes, you generate positive momentum and reinforce everyone's long-term commitment.

- Trust God for the outcomes. Don't be impatient. When change is rushed, it can increase resistance and be extremely expensive. However, when leaders allow change to happen more naturally, it tends to be slower but it also receives greater acceptance. Build alliances and take the time to show people the benefits of moving ahead.

- Encourage people constantly. Once people start moving down a new path, they need frequent encouragement, especially when they encounter the inevitable obstacles, unexpected disasters and the uncharted forks in the road.

The initial first wins will not bring everyone in the organization on board. People adopt change at different rates.[15] But the initial small wins will be instrumental in bringing a critical mass of people on board with the vision.

How to Improve

The following are some practical ways that you can improve in this area of leadership:

- What do you believe? Clarify your own core values by listing them and then sharing them with your constituents.

- Ask others on your team to do the same. Resolve any incompatibilities.

---

[15] Please see *Understanding Change: SpiritBuilt Leadership #7* by Malcolm Webber for more on this.

- Keep track of how you spend your time and your money. Do it for a month. Check to see whether your actions are consistent with your values. If there are inconsistencies, determine what you need to do to align your actions with your values.

- Learn to say "yes" when something lines up with your priorities even if it is not convenient at the time. Learn to say "no" when something does not match your values, even though it might seem like a good idea. If you are serious about your values you will say "yes" and "no" with conviction and consistency.

- Ask your team members frequently about their own lives and whether their actions are lining up with their values.

- Tell stories about people in the church or ministry who live up to their biblical values, especially when they do so at personal cost.

- When you make commitments write them in your daily planner. Keep your promises.

- Set goals that are achievable. Clearly inform the people about these goals as well as key milestones, so they can easily see their progress.

- Focus on the little things – not only on the big things – so that people know you value the quality of their work.

- Expose yourself to the life stories of great Christian leaders, especially those who suffered for their faith. Learn from them.

- Ask your friends who they think are the most credible people they know. Talk to these people if possible. Ask them for advice and input. Spend time with them.

- Make yourself genuinely accountable to someone you trust. Give that person unconditional permission to challenge you regarding consistency in your life and work.

BIBLICAL EXERCISES

1. Find examples in both testaments of leaders who personally set the example.

2. Find examples in both testaments of leaders who built a consensus of shared values before moving forward.

3. Find examples in both testaments of leaders who broke the vision down and started with some small wins.

chapter 6

Leaders Sustain the Vision

Leadership consists of helping someone move from where he is now to somewhere else. Along this journey there will be obstacles and failures, and other inducements to give up. Like Israel in the wilderness, the people will often complain and want to "go back to Egypt."

This brings us to the final practice of exemplary leaders: leaders sustain the vision by strengthening the hearts of the people. Leaders keep the fire burning. By keeping the people focused on the ultimate goal, by affirming them and their contributions and by celebrating their accomplishments, leaders keep their people "moving" in the right direction until the vision is fulfilled.

Focus on the Ultimate Goal

Christian leaders should always take the long view. We are striving towards eternity, not merely temporal goals. By keeping the people focused on our ultimate destination, we can encourage them to endure the many sufferings and setbacks along the way.

> *Therefore we do not lose heart. Though outwardly we are wasting away, yet inwardly we are being renewed day by day. For our light and momentary troubles are achieving for us an eternal glory that far outweighs them all. So we fix our eyes not on what is seen, but on what is unseen. For what is seen is temporary, but what is unseen is eternal. (2 Cor. 4:16-18)*

> *Let us not become weary in doing good, for at the proper time we will reap a harvest if we do not give up. (Gal. 6:9)*

> *Praise be to the God and Father of our Lord Jesus Christ! In his great mercy he has given us new birth into a living hope through the resurrection of Jesus Christ from the dead, and into an inheritance that can never perish, spoil or fade – kept in heaven for you, who through faith are shielded by God's power until the coming of the salvation that is ready to be revealed in the last time. In this you greatly rejoice, though now for a little while you may have had to suffer grief in all kinds of trials. These have come so that your faith – of greater worth than gold, which perishes even though refined by fire – may be proved genuine and may result in praise, glory and honor when Jesus Christ is revealed. (1 Pet. 1:3-7)*

> *but he who stands firm to the end will be saved. (Matt. 24:13)*

> *Now there is in store for me the crown of righteousness, which the Lord, the righteous Judge, will award to me on that day – and not only to me, but also to all who have longed for his appearing. (2 Tim. 4:8)*

The future is why we keep going now through difficulties and struggles. In the end, it will be worth it all!

The Power of Affirmation

Effective leaders affirm their people and their contributions.[16] Look at how Paul wrote to the Corinthian church:

> *I do not say this to condemn you; I have said before that you have such a place in our hearts that we would live or die with you. I have*

---

[16] Gary Chapman, in *The Five Love Languages*, identifies five specific ways to affirm another person: gifts, acts of service, words of affirmation, quality time and physical touch.

> *great confidence in you; I take great pride in you.*[17] *I am greatly encouraged; in all our troubles my joy knows no bounds… I am glad I can have complete confidence in you. (2 Cor. 7:3-4, 16)*

Paul's words are even more significant when we consider that this was the same church that previously required extensive correction in 1 Corinthians. Thus, leaders should not only affirm people who are perfect! Even in 1 Corinthians, before beginning his correction, Paul was positive toward the people:

> *I always thank God for you because of his grace given you in Christ Jesus. For in him you have been enriched in every way – in all your speaking and in all your knowledge – because our testimony about Christ was confirmed in you. Therefore you do not lack any spiritual gift as you eagerly wait for our Lord Jesus Christ to be revealed. He will keep you strong to the end, so that you will be blameless on the day of our Lord Jesus Christ. (1 Cor. 1:4-8)*

Prior to his correction of the Colossians, Paul spoke affirmation:

> *We always thank God, the Father of our Lord Jesus Christ, when we pray for you, because we have heard of your faith in Christ Jesus and of the love you have for all the saints – the faith and love that spring from the hope that is stored up for you in heaven and that you have already heard about in the word of truth, the gospel that has come to you. All over the world this gospel is bearing fruit and growing, just as it has been doing among you since the day you heard it and understood God's grace in all its truth. You learned it from Epaphras, our dear fellow servant, who is a faithful minister of Christ on our behalf, and who also told us of your love in the Spirit. (Col. 1:3-8)*

Thus, affirmation is not based upon the perfection of the people receiving it, but upon the grace and love of God.

---

[17] Paul was not proud of himself – that is sin (Jam. 4:6). He was proud of others – that is "biblically acceptable pride."

Even in the midst of his stern rebuke to the Galatians, Paul is still genuine in his affirmation:

> *My dear children, for whom I am again in the pains of childbirth until Christ is formed in you, (Gal. 4:19)*
>
> *You were running a good race. Who cut in on you and kept you from obeying the truth? (Gal. 5:7)*

Paul's letters are characterized by affectionate affirmation that is heartfelt, sincere, specific, and, most importantly, expressed:

> *First, I thank my God through Jesus Christ for all of you, because your faith is being reported all over the world. God, whom I serve with my whole heart in preaching the gospel of his Son, is my witness how constantly I remember you in my prayers at all times; and I pray that now at last by God's will the way may be opened for me to come to you. I long to see you… (Rom. 1:8-11)*
>
> *For this reason, ever since I heard about your faith in the Lord Jesus and your love for all the saints, I have not stopped giving thanks for you, remembering you in my prayers. (Eph. 1:15-16)*
>
> *I thank my God every time I remember you. In all my prayers for all of you, I always pray with joy because of your partnership in the gospel from the first day until now, being confident of this, that he who began a good work in you will carry it on to completion until the day of Christ Jesus. It is right for me to feel this way about all of you, since I have you in my heart; for whether I am in chains or defending and confirming the gospel, all of you share in God's grace with me. God can testify how I long for all of you with the affection of Christ Jesus. (Phil. 1:3- 8)*
>
> *We always thank God for all of you, mentioning you in our prayers. We continually remember before our God and Father your work produced by faith, your labor prompted by love, and your endurance*

inspired by hope in our Lord Jesus Christ. For we know, brothers loved by God, that he has chosen you, (1 Thess. 1:2-4)

As apostles of Christ we could have been a burden to you, but we were gentle among you, like a mother caring for her little children. We loved you so much that we were delighted to share with you not only the gospel of God but our lives as well, because you had become so dear to us. (1 Thess. 2:7-8)

And we also thank God continually because, when you received the word of God, which you heard from us, you accepted it not as the word of men, but as it actually is, the word of God, which is at work in you who believe. (1 Thess. 2:13)

How can we thank God enough for you in return for all the joy we have in the presence of our God because of you? (1 Thess. 3:9)

We ought always to thank God for you, brothers, and rightly so, because your faith is growing more and more, and the love every one of you has for each other is increasing. Therefore, among God's churches we boast about your perseverance and faith in all the persecutions and trials you are enduring. (2 Thess. 1:3-4)

thank God, whom I serve, as my forefathers did, with a clear conscience, as night and day I constantly remember you in my prayers. Recalling your tears, I long to see you, so that I may be filled with joy. I have been reminded of your sincere faith, which first lived in your grandmother Lois and in your mother Eunice and, I am persuaded, now lives in you also. (2 Tim. 1:3-5)

I always thank my God as I remember you in my prayers, because I hear about your faith in the Lord Jesus and your love for all the saints. I pray that you may be active in sharing your faith, so that you will have a full understanding of every good thing we have in Christ. Your love has given me great joy and encouragement, because you, brother, have refreshed the hearts of the saints. (Philem. 4-7)

John also affirmed the people he led:

> *It gave me great joy to have some brothers come and tell about your faithfulness to the truth and how you continue to walk in the truth. I have no greater joy than to hear that my children are walking in the truth. Dear friend, you are faithful in what you are doing for the brothers, even though they are strangers to you. They have told the church about your love. You will do well to send them on their way in a manner worthy of God. (3 John 3-6)*

Of course, Paul and John were only following in the footsteps of God the Father who affirmed His Son:

> *As soon as Jesus was baptized, he went up out of the water. At that moment heaven was opened, and he saw the Spirit of God descending like a dove and lighting on him. And a voice from heaven said, "This is my Son, whom I love; with him I am well pleased." (Matt. 3:16-17)*

God is the ultimate Affirmer. Thus, it is only natural that those who are united with Him should do so too. Our inability to give healthy affirmation to others is a revelation of our own spiritual poverty.

Such affirmation is genuine encouragement. It should not be flattery, which only puffs up and "works ruin":

> *A lying tongue hates those it hurts, and a flattering mouth works ruin. (Prov. 26:28)*

> *Whoever flatters his neighbor is spreading a net for his feet. (Prov. 29:5)*

Flattery is deceitful. One who flatters another deliberately tries to manipulate him, attempting to get something out of him by "buttering him up." This is quite different from affirmation which is truthful and sincere with no manipulate motive.

To be effective, affirmation must be:

- Sincere. It must be from the heart. People will sense when it's genuine. Moreover, people can develop a cynical attitude about excessive praise from above and infer that it may just be a tool to manipulate them into working harder.

- Specific. Like the biblical leaders, we should share specific encouragement, not only generalities that could apply to anyone. Moreover, affirmation should be made in the second person ("you have...") and be shared personally.

- Spoken (or written). Positive thoughts or feelings are not enough; we must communicate them to others.

It is difficult for many people to give sincere affirmation to others for several possible reasons:

- We live in a negative, critical culture. It is much easier to be cynical than affirming.

- By nature, man is self-absorbed. He often does not notice the contributions of others. He does, however, notice when others do things that cut across his own agenda, thus eliciting his displeasure and rebuke.

- By nature, man is proud and self-loving. He would rather receive praise than give it.

- Leaders – especially in the Western world – tend to underestimate the importance that people attach to positive feedback and to overestimate the value of formal rewards.

Christian leaders must have the courage to swim against the cultural current and to give healthy affirmation to others. People need affirmation and encouragement. As someone said, "We live by encouragement and we die without it; slowly, sadly, angrily."

This is how effective leaders keep the people moving ahead, rather than by threats, demands or coercion.

Recognizing Contributions

Leaders cannot assume their constituents know when they've done a good job or that they're appreciated; leaders must recognize contributions. People need encouragement as they persist in their journey to fulfill the vision, and they need it frequently. People need to hear that they are doing well and that their efforts are appreciated. This is the leader's role: to encourage the hearts of the people.

In recognizing contributions, leaders will:

- Recognize that we all are serving God. It is Him we all will stand before one day, and if we serve Him from our hearts, we will hear the words, "Well done, good and faithful servant!" (Matt. 25:21). Our ultimate rewards for faithfulness are in eternity. Nevertheless, leaders should not use this as an excuse to deny temporal encouragement to their people.

- Build confidence through high expectations. Leaders' belief in others creates a self-fulfilling prophecy: people act in ways that are consistent with their leader's expectations of them. Leaders who truly believe in their constituents and who express that confidence through high expectations are able to bring out the very best in their people.

    A cheerful look brings joy to the heart… (Prov. 15:30)

> *When a king's face brightens, it means life; his favor is like a rain cloud in spring. (Prov. 16:15)*

- Connect performance with rewards. "The worker deserves his wages" (1 Tim. 5:18). People avoid behavior that is punished, repeat behavior that is rewarded and eventually drop behavior that is ignored. Therefore, if long hours and hard work are not noticed, people will soon feel that they are taken for granted, and may decrease their efforts. When connecting performance with rewards, leaders should be sure that people know exactly what is expected of them, provide frequent feedback along the way, and reward only those who meet the standards.

- Use a variety of rewards. The creative use of rewards is a defining characteristic of good leadership. Leaders should use both intrinsic rewards (that are built into the work itself, such as job satisfaction, praise and thank-you notes) and extrinsic rewards (such as material remuneration and promotions). The enthusiasm and motivation of the people will be increased if the reward and recognition system is designed participatively. Finally, peer-, or subordinate-recognition systems can be highly effective. In Proverbs 31, the virtuous woman receives praise from others as a part of her reward:

  > *Charm is deceptive, and beauty is fleeting; but a woman who fears the LORD is to be praised. Give her the reward she has earned, and let her works bring her praise at the city gate. (Prov. 31:30-31)*

- Be instant in season and out of season. The reward should be given as soon after the accomplishment as possible, so it is directly connected with it. The leader himself should proactively look for people who are doing the right things, and then personally present their reward to show his appreciation, making very specific mention of the reason for the reward.

- Make recognition public. Public recognition promotes the individual as a model for others to emulate; thus, everyone learns what the right things to do are. Public recognition also empowers the recipients by increasing their visibility.

    Give her the reward she has earned, and let her works bring her praise at the city gate. (Prov. 31:31)

    In Proverbs 31, God says to praise the virtuous woman "at the city gate." In ancient cities, the city gate was one of the "highest traffic" areas in the whole city! Jesus practiced this – He commended people with others around (e.g., Matt. 8:10; 16:17-20; Luke 7:44-50).

- Be disciplined with your affirmations. Make it your constant practice. One executive made this a routine by placing five coins in his pocket at the beginning of each day and then moving one coin to the other pocket each time he complimented an employee. In another case, a restaurant owner whose schedule was too hectic to recognize his staff during work hours took a few minutes after closing time to jot personal notes to those who made a real difference that day.

- Be interminably positive and hopeful. Through their encouragement, leaders give their people the courage to endure the tough times and to win great victories. But they must not wait until the final victory is won before encouraging their people. Leaders should build up their constituents all along the way. God does that to us!

Delivering Correction

In addition to communicating positive feedback, leaders also have to share negative things with their constituents at times. When delivering correction or "constructive criticism," leaders should do the following:[18]

- Pray first. The leader should ask for God's help and wisdom so that he can speak with the appropriate spirit and with the right words. He also should pray for the person receiving the correction so he can receive it with humility and grace.

    Reckless words pierce like a sword, but the tongue of the wise brings healing. (Prov. 12:18)

    A man of knowledge uses words with restraint, and a man of understanding is even-tempered. (Prov. 17:27)

- Do it privately. To publicly criticize someone's work or behavior is to humiliate them. Sometimes it can even lead to unnecessary lawsuits. Contrary to praise, which should be offered publicly whenever possible, discussions about someone's deficiencies should remain private.[19]

- Do it personally. It is often a mistake to deliver a correction by phone. It is always a mistake to do it via email. On a telephone call, the person still has the benefit of hearing the tone of your voice, even if they can't see you; but email is absolutely without any non-verbal assistance whatsoever! Face-to-face conversations allow the leader to observe the person's non-verbal language (which is often far more revealing than what is spoken). This may assist the leader in the sometimes arduous task of identifying root problems. Similarly, a personal

---

[18] Some of these ideas have been adapted from *Management by Proverbs* by Michael A. Zigarelli.
[19] Exceptional circumstances are described in 1 Tim. 5:20.

discussion permits the person to more clearly observe the leader's concern both for him and for the whole organization.

- Begin with something positive. Researchers have found that people are more likely to accept negative feedback as accurate if some positive feedback is offered first. It is essential that the person understand that his leader sees not just his deficiencies, but also his contributions to the organization. At the same time, if *significant* affirmation is due the person, then it's probably best to deliver it at a separate time. Appending a "but on the other hand…" to an affirmation often has the effect of nullifying its beneficial aspects.

- Get to the point. Most people can sense when their leader has a problem with them. So, when the leader beats around the bush, it is both transparent and frustrating for the person receiving the correction.

- Speak in terms of "I," not "you." Speaking in the first person is a good way to minimize defensiveness. A statement like, "I don't understand your behavior in this situation" is easier to receive than the blunt "You're doing something wrong." The first approach communicates essentially the same information, but it runs less risk of creating defensiveness.

> *A gentle answer turns away wrath, but a harsh word stirs up anger. (Prov. 15:1)*

- Be specific. Generalized or abstract criticisms (e.g., "You're doing poorly") do not work as well as more specific feedback. Be clear about what is expected and contrast that with objective facts about what the person has or has not accomplished. The leader must clearly identify this gap between his expectations and the person's current performance, thus bringing into sharp focus the problem that must be addressed. This will become the basis for a more constructive discussion of how to bridge that gap.

- Stick to the facts. Be objective and avoid speculative judgments about the causes of misbehavior or under-performance. Instead ask the person about the reasons for their behavior or performance and then actively listen to their response.

- Don't twist the knife. In any one discussion, there is no need to repeat criticisms. The person will usually get the idea. Furthermore, if possible, only deal with one problem per conversation and avoid resurrecting old problems that were previously resolved. People tend to perceive such bringing up of the past as unnecessary and unfair.

- Jointly craft a solution. After presenting the negative feedback, involve the person in solving the problem. Someone who has helped craft a solution is usually more committed to it than one who has a solution forced upon him. Pinpoint the problem and set up some mutually agreeable goals as a standard against which to evaluate future performance. Also, if appropriate, jointly design a development plan to train the person in his areas of need.

- Follow up. After the plan for improvement has been made and agreed upon, the leader must hold the person accountable for his future actions. If there is no lasting change, more drastic measures may be necessary.

- Offer feedback continuously. Feedback should be given more than once or twice a year. Ideally, when a leader sees a person doing something wrong (or right), he should let him know about it immediately to correct (or reinforce) the behavior.

Celebrating Accomplishments

Accomplishing great things through organizations is hard work. To keep hope and determination alive, leaders recognize the contributions their people make. And because every winning team needs to share in the rewards of their corporate efforts, leaders celebrate accomplishments. Effective leaders are cheerleaders; they make everyone a part of the victory. Encouraging the heart does not only involve recognizing individual achievements; it also means celebrating the efforts of the entire group.

In various ways, the Old Testament saints built memorials to the great works of God. Here are some examples:

> *Moses built an altar and called it The Lord is my Banner. (Ex. 17:15)*

> *Because the Lord kept vigil that night to bring them out of Egypt, on this night all the Israelites are to keep vigil to honor the Lord for the generations to come. (Ex. 12:42)*

> *(Therefore these days were called Purim, from the word pur.) Because of everything written in this letter and because of what they had seen and what had happened to them, the Jews took it upon themselves to establish the custom that they and their descendants and all who join them should without fail observe these two days every year, in the way prescribed and at the time appointed. These days should be remembered and observed in every generation by every family, and in every province and in every city. And these days of Purim should never cease to be celebrated by the Jews, nor should the memory of them die out among their descendants. (Esther 9:26-28)*

The saints stopped and rehearsed the faithful works of God and built something to signify them and to remind them of God's faithfulness in the future.

The New Testament church also had celebrations during the Communion of the Bread and Cup (1 Cor. 11:23-34) and also during their "love feasts" (2 Pet. 2:13; Jude 12). These were times of joyful celebration of the unity of the saints and their salvation by God.

Leaders should do this in their organizations. They should frequently pause and rehearse some of the victories God has given them. It is so easy in our fast paced society to rush past the faithfulness of God, and to just take it for granted. We need to pause and build memorials to the faithfulness of God to our organizations. In celebrating team accomplishments, leaders will:

- Celebrate the right things. Celebrations should call attention to and reinforce key organizational values. This will let others know what is valued. Moreover, there must be consistency between what the leader espouses and what he celebrates. The celebration must be an honest expression of commitment to certain key values and to the hard and sacrificial work of the people who have lived those values.

- Involve everyone and celebrate publicly. The public nature of celebrations makes people's actions more visible to others and helps to bond the people together as a team.

- Schedule regular celebrations. Some celebrations should be spontaneous, but leaders should also have certain organizational celebrations at the same time each year. Nations do this to remind their people of their common struggles, sacrifices, legacies and continuing responsibilities to each other. As a minimum, each organization should have at least one celebration each year that involves everyone.

- Join in the celebration. Celebrations are great times for leaders to personally connect with their constituents, creating a commonness ("we're all in this together") as well as a deeper level of shared vision, values and experiences. The leader does not necessarily have to lead the celebration, but he should participate in it.

- Have fun. Without having some fun sometimes, few people will be able to handle the level of intensity and hard work required for high achievement. Researchers have found a significant relationship between fun and productivity! So, lighten up; enjoy life a little!

- Create social support networks. Supportive relationships are critically important to maintain personal and organizational vitality. Through celebrating accomplishments, leaders help create these networks of relationships. As organizational members interact on more than just a professional level, their personal relationships are nurtured and they will grow in their love and caring for each other. Furthermore, without group celebrations, it is easy for individuals to believe that the organization revolves around their individual work. Thus, celebrations reinforce the truth that we are all dependent on, and responsible for, one other (1 Cor. 12:14-26).

- Stay passionate. Of all the things that sustain a leader over time, love is the most enduring – his love for God and for the people he's leading. Through celebrations, the leader can communicate this love to his people, and a passion communicated can be a passion personally embraced.

How to Improve

The following are some practical ways that you can improve in this area of leadership:

- Make a list of specific ways that you can recognize others and celebrate accomplishments in your church or ministry. Think of things such as:

- Catching people doing something right.
- Being creative with rewards.
- Recognizing others in public.
- Personalizing rewards.
- Increasing responsibility and opening new doors of opportunity.
- Giving people personal attention and time.
- Consistently supporting them.
- Telling the story of everyone's corporate achievements.

- Plan a celebration of some kind for each small milestone that your team reaches. Don't wait until the whole project is finished to celebrate.

- Tell a public story about one person in the organization who exceeded expectations.

- Involve others in designing reward and recognition systems.

- Encourage all your people to recognize accomplishments of all kinds. Create a culture in which peers recognize peers.

- Say "thank you" when you appreciate something someone does.

- Write thank-you cards, notes, emails. Establish a discipline of writing two or three each week. People will never complain about being thanked too much, but they will complain about being thanked too little.

- Provide quick feedback about results. Feedback can range from a simple "well done" to a detailed debriefing session on how the project went and what everyone learned through it.

- Be personally involved. If you don't attend celebration events, you're sending a message that it's not important to you.

- Set aside one day each year as a special organizational-celebration day. Nations do this and it's very effective in building national loyalty and a sense of patriotism and belonging. Churches and ministries should do it too.

- Find people who have a reputation for helping others to develop. Ask them how they encourage others to excel.

BIBLICAL EXERCISES

1. Find examples in both testaments of leaders who kept their people focused on the ultimate goal.

2. Find examples in both testaments of leaders who affirmed their people and their contributions.

3. Find examples in both testaments of leaders who celebrated their people's accomplishments.

These five practices of exemplary leaders are summarized in the following table:

Practice	What the leader does	The leader's actions related to the vision	The leader's actions related to the people	The leader's actions related to the three parts of leadership
1 Fire-starters	The leader goes to the mountain with God, dreams dreams and sees visions of the future.	Sees the vision	Clearly sees their future potential and purpose.	1
2 Fire-throwers	The leader comes down from the mountain and shares the vision he's seen with his people in such a way that they clearly see it and passionately own it.	Shares the vision	Engages their hearts with the vision of their own futures.	2
3 Fire-builders	The leader builds a team that will take responsibility for practically acting on the vision and bringing it to pass.	Shifts the vision	Builds them into a team and enables them to act on the vision and make it happen.	3
4 Fire-eaters	The leader demonstrates that the vision will work by personally modeling it and by starting with small wins.	Shows the vision	Sets them the example of his own model and builds credibility that the vision will work.	3

5 Fire-stokers	The leader encourages the people to pursue the vision by focusing on the ultimate goal, by recognizing contributions and by celebrating accomplishments.	Sustains the vision	Strengthens and encourages them to continue to act and ultimately bring the vision for their futures to pass.	3

Books in the *SpiritBuilt Leadership* Series
by Malcolm Webber, Ph.D.

1. *Leadership.* Deals with the nature of leadership, servant leadership, and other basic leadership issues.

2. *Healthy Leaders.* Presents a simple but effective model of what constitutes a healthy Christian leader.

3. *Leading.* A study of the practices of exemplary leaders.

4. *Building Leaders.* Leaders build leaders! However, leader development is highly complex and very little understood. This book examines core principles of leader development.

5. *Leaders & Managers.* Deals with the distinctions between leaders and managers. Contains extensive worksheets.

6. *Abusive Leadership.* A must read for all Christian leaders. Reveals the true natures and sources of abusive leadership and servant leadership.

7. *Understanding Change.* Leading change is one of the most difficult leadership responsibilities. It is also one of the most important. This book is an excellent primer that will help you understand resistance to change, the change process and how to help people through change.

8. *Building Teams.* What teams are and how they best work.

9. *Understanding Organizations.* A primer on organizational structure.

10. *Women in Leadership.* A biblical study concerning this very controversial issue.

11. ***Healthy Followers.*** The popular conception that "everything depends on leaders" is not entirely correct. Without thoughtful and active followers, the greatest of leaders will fail. This book studies the characteristics of healthy followers and is also a great resource for team building.

12. ***Listening.*** Listening is one of the most important of all leadership skills. This book studies how we can be better listeners and better leaders.

13. ***Transformational Thinking.*** This book introduces a new model of transformational thinking – of loving God with our minds – that identifies the critical thinking capacities of a healthy Christian leader. In addition, practical ways of nurturing those thinking capacities are described.

Strategic Press
www.StrategicPress.org

Strategic Press is a division of Strategic Global Assistance, Inc.
www.sgai.org

513 S. Main St. Suite 2
Elkhart, IN 46516
U.S.A

+1-844-532-3371 (LEADER-1)

www.ingramcontent.com/pod-product-compliance
Lightning Source LLC
LaVergne TN
LVHW051848080426
835512LV00018B/3142